Saluda Reflections

poems by

Arthur Turfa

Finishing Line Press
Georgetown, Kentucky

Saluda Reflections

Copyright © 2018 by Arthur Turfa
ISBN 978-1-63534-547-6 First Edition
All rights reserved under International and Pan-American Copyright Conventions. No part of this book may be reproduced in any manner whatsoever without written permission from the publisher, except in the case of brief quotations embodied in critical articles and reviews.

ACKNOWLEDGMENTS

"While Gazing at the Water", was previously published in *Our Poetry Archive,* 1 April 2017, http://ourpoetryarchive.blogspot.com/2017/04/arthur-turfa.html
"One Morning You Will Decide" was previously published in MUSED Bella Online Volume 11, Issue 1, Spring 2017 http://www.bellaonline.com/review/issues/spring2017/p031.html
"Corvinus" was published in *Whispers*, 30 June 2016, http://whispersinthewind333.blogspot.com/2016/06/corvinus-by-arthur-turfa-united-states.html

Some of these poems existed as my first two books came together, but for one reason or another, did not fit into either manuscript. They cover the scope of my career, and some deal with earlier events and themes. A few of them deal with some contemporary issues. All of them found expression in the woods of Saluda County, South Carolina.

I am indebted to my fellow poets Joanna Kurowska, Martha Magenta, Alicia Salabert and Len Lawson for their friendship and support.

Publisher: Leah Maines
Editor: Christen Kincaid
Cover Art and Design: Carol Worthington-Levy
Author Photo: Pamela Chesser Turfa

Printed in the USA on acid-free paper.
Order online: www.finishinglinepress.com
     also available on amazon.com

Author inquiries and mail orders:
Finishing Line Press
P. O. Box 1626
Georgetown, Kentucky 40324
U. S. A.

Table of Contents

Giles County Sonnets 1981-1984 1
Wyoming Valley, Pennsylvania 3
Reflection on Musgrove Mill and Today 4
Recollections of Berkeley 5
Morning in Exeter 6
At the Bundestag Cafeteria 7
Poisonous Fumes over Donora 8
At the Rosewood Arts and Music Festival 9
The Twelve Bridges Road 10
In Memory of W. Carter Merbreier 12
The Transfiguration of Cap'n Douglas 13
Corvinus 15
Her Eyes 16
The Woman Who Knew Aldous Huxley 17
One Morning You Will Decide 19
The Archipelago 20
Aubade: The Bather 21
While Gazing at the Water 22
The Sullen Expression of Growing Anger 23
Idyll: The Shepherd and His Muse on Parnassus
    Reflecting on the 2016 Election 25
We Will Not Hear Words Like that Again 26
The House on the Ridge 27
Sonnet for All Saints Day 28
E'en's Last Dark Hour 29
Lingering at Castalia 30
On Hearing Rachel Portman's "Cider House Rules" 31

for Holden

Giles County Sonnets 1981-1984

1
Westward flows second-oldest river,
meandering among forests, mountains
and several scattered communities
strewn throughout elevations that can bring
both snowfall and relief from summer heat.
Wide valleys extend to reveal autumn's
splendor or springtime's greening radiance.
In midyear came I, crossing the ridge that
divided states which once had been one,
coming to the county seat, near the plant
upon which all of our fortunes were fixed.
Full of visions and dreams, here I tried
to fashion them into realities
and make the hills resound with hosannas.

2
Two paths to the Cascades, the waterfalls
on the verge of the Appalachian chain:
to the right, a rising, falling way o'er
boulders, narrow, winding slippery trail.
To the left, a graded, easier slope
usually taken for our returning.
Newcomers to the county ritually
walk, later leading others the same way
to behold sound and sight of waterfalls.
In time I walked with the one with whom I
would walk on trails more arduous but on
easier paths as well, going very
far beyond the branched canopy of
the ways leading to and from the Cascades.

3
Over the years, a few places remain
fixed solidly in my mind. A high hill
overlooking apple orchards, farmhouse
full of laughter, and widening valley.
A flower-ringed homestead near a cottage,
untouched grandeur spread over horizons
or as close by as a bend in the road.
Newspaper office not far from courthouse
as afternoon shadows settled in,
conversations beyond all temporal
pressures, wisdom and laughter mingling.
Parsonage softened from monastic state,
precursor of what was would in time follow
in a half-dozen different places.

4
One sunny late May afternoon first I
saw Angel's Rest looming proudly above
the town. Beyond it, that very weekend,
a misfit murdered two hikers on the
Appalachian Trail. My future love
would cover the trial, but we did not meet.
That year bloomed my life in early season,
my destiny for several short years
spent between the ridges of this valley
with hazy visions of what was beyond.
Twelve months after slaying, memorial
made at hikers' hostel. Afterwards, some
bourbon with a bishop and a colleague
as the sun set over West Virginia.

Wyoming Valley, Pennsylvania

From the sloping yard on Welsh Hill,
I look across the Susquehanna, the
green hills leaping like playful lambs
until they evolve into the Endless Mountains.

Around me the fading coal town, ringed
by silent breakers from the mines that
lured thousands here. Below untouched
anthracite and a honeycomb of shafts
hinder doors and cabinets as they are shut.

What happens to the work ethic when
mines and mills close, when some of the
young people conduct a second immigration
for a job with benefits but most linger until
a relative bequeaths them half a double?
Some turn to drink, others to drugs, too many
immerse themselves in waves of negativity.

The river flows towards Chesapeake Bay,
past communities but a show of what they were
and also of what they might still be. From atop
a mountain I later watched until one cold February
took me an ocean away to my second home.

Reflection on Musgrove Mill and Today

Along the Enoree's banks, Musgrove Mill
lies among the Piedmont's pines and hardwoods.
On a sultry, long-ago August day
Loyalist and Patriot joined battle,
neighbors and kinsman clashing, Scotsmen too,
blood flowing on green-ringed forest meadow.
Now rages renewed warfare all around
in cyberspace, chatrooms, and face-to-face.
Everyone a combatant now, none are spared;
Tarleton's Quarter appears merciful.
Friendships severed, relationships broken
not only here but from coast-to-coast.
The Republic for which for which the victors bled
unravels like a second-hand overcoat.

Recollections of Berkeley

Not long for the Bay
sitting for two hours
during the Spring Quarter,
learning about long ago
slowly sensed I
to connect with something
beyond the current miasma,
my options as limited
as land ending at the Pacific Coast.

Choices emerged several blocks
from where I existed.
One slightly familiar to me,
the other less so.
Choosing the former
at chapel seeing
ancient and modern mingling:
guitar liturgy, pottery chalice
offering viaticum for decades.

Through the years
gradually realizing
the other place found me
and welcomed me.

A Morning in Exeter

Past rooms of tourists and bedsitters
I head toward the stairs, descending
to an empty breakfast room adjacent
a bustling, bacon-scented kitchen.
Once outside on softly-sunlit streets
barely touched by traffic I walk
until concrete gives way to grass
In front of Devonshire stones
forming the Cathedral of St. Peter
reflecting rays of rising sun.

From the other side of the grounds
an old man wearing a kilt approaches,
Within moments we meet in the Lady Chapel
for sacramental solace, stripped of music.
Warmed by glowing stained glass
as if nothing else existed.
His throaty brogue wishes me good morning
as I pass the pews and monuments
toward busier than before streets,
returning as tourists and bedsitters
fill the breakfast room adjacent
to the bustling bacon-scented kitchen.

At the Bundestag Canteen

Sunlight fills the space
as staffers and guests
pause at midday.

Between my bites of
Spaghetti Bolognese
I look outside
 down toward green spaces
 meant to remain unmarked
 and remember
 another who ate
 a meatless version
 on his last day

*"Oh Arthur, only you
would ever know that"*
my friend tells me.

Soon I shepherd the
group to *Potsdamer Platz*
for some shopping.

As shadows fall we
retrace the rails
returning to the Sauerland.

Poisonous Fumes over Donora

With Dewey leading the October polls,
yellow sulfurous smog wafted from the
steel mills along the Monongahela,
shrouding Donora's steep hills, killing some
quickly, more later on, even filling
the infant lungs of my elder brother,
partially assuring no trip to Nam.

Truman won in an upset, Donora's
stalwart Democrats remaining loyal.
The mills ran three shifts for a while longer
until the sons of immigrants needed
to seek new homes or new careers themselves.

Almost three-score and ten years afterward,
an orange smog rolled in, just as toxic,
but slower-acting. Millionaire Messiah
promising flourishing mines and mills to
those who remained amid faded glories;
Clinton's firewall crumbled in November,
grandchildren of immigrants scorning her.
When she lost Pennsylvania, another
smog settled over my mind, and I said
what my grandfather would say: *Yohe Isten!*
The orange smog would not dissipate soon.

At the Rosewood Art and Music Festival

Standing in morning sunlight
young girl reading my poem
about Parnassus. Her mother
beside her, both hearing about
the Muse-loved mountain and
Castalia's cleansing, inspiring
streams. Mother and daughter,
eyes aglow: Do they behold the
graceful dance of the Muses?

Several hours pass- hikers fresh
From Virginian trails ask me
to read a poem of my choice.
I read "Three Woods" and we
find ourselves transported to
places long-loved and never-
forgotten. We stand on the
parking lot and feel sylvan
coolness and mossy ground
under entwining branches
reaching above us. Such
is verse's power and glory.

The Twelve Bridges Road

If you are going to the eccentric place
you travel the Twelve Bridges Road;
some of them span a creek
or a tributary stream
but the one over the Broad River
stretches out in the sunlight,
a slender ribbon between
widely-separated bluffs.

Coming from the old place
the route was shorter
but not as interesting.
Flatness between fields
punctuated by crossroads.
But now out of friendship
and a sort of obligation
I travel the Twelve Bridges Road

Not being told some things,
but expected to know them.
Not being told other things,
because I am not in the loop,
I offer pieces of the puzzle
but some are working on it
with pieces unknown to me
in clandestine conversations
while I am on the Twelve Bridges Road.

At some point you must realize
the road only goes so far.
Eventually you sense that
there are other roads to travel
and that you will never
resolve the enigma.

Since then I have never traveled
along the Twelve Bridges Road
through forest and crossroad
across streams, the North Tyger
or descended from the ridge
downward toward the Broad River.

Other roads delight me
and I roam to different places.

In Memoriam: W. Carter Merbreier
> *Pastor and then Children's TV Show Host,*
> *Predecessor at my parish in Philadelphia*

In catacomb-like basement, bright
patches of color from the time
when children thronged Sunday School.
He and his wife painted all of that.

Chancel bathed in colored light
as liturgy became drama; strapped to
a cross preaching on Good Friday.
On Palm Sunday he rode a donkey down the aisle

Taking program north on Broad Street
In time for White Flight to decimate
the membership: blame descended on him.
There were policemen in the Legion of Cornelius

Ecclesiastical rigidity transformed Pastor
into Cap'n Noah on a score of TV markets
with puppet shows and bright-colored sets.
He's still on Channel 6

The Transfiguration of Cap'n Douglas

We waited by the river where there was no station
about half an hour after the workday ended.
Cap'n Douglas heading home, I had a date.
Pulling a small bottle from a pocket, the Cap'n
swigged something light brown. Smiling, he said
*"If I had brandy, I'd offer you some, but you is
a college man."* In reply I smiled and shrugged.

In the cement plant the Cap'n operated a dryer,
working both ends himself. Arthritic back pointing
the opposite way than his Phillies cigar, this
septuagenarian Geechie outworked us all.

Soon the train slowed down to receive us.
The Cap'n tossed an empty small bottle
as an offering to the woods, then bounded aboard.
The conductors knew him by name.

Full of hot, tired commuters, the train headed east
like a sauna between the tracks.
The Cap'n and the conductors carried on
while I looked at the Schuylkill and pondered the date.

After a few minutes rose the Cap'n, steadying himself
against the rear wall, and shouted out the stations
as a commanding general addressing troops
or someone dispensing eternal wisdom:
MIQUON, IVY RIDGE, WISSAHICKSON NEXT STATION STOP
above the noise of the train and the shuffle of feet,
perhaps saying everything that he could not say
while running his machine, while heading North long ago,
scraping an existence from the Labor Pool
on 4th and Girard and Resco Products, Incorporated.
I looked away from the river and marveled
at the man I saw in a different way.

Before North Philadelphia Station I got ready
to catch the connection to Center City.
I said goodbye to the Cap'n, receiving a quick yellow-toothed smile
before he cried to the universe
 NORTH PHILADELPHIA NEXT STATION STOP

Corvinus

History books generally ignored
Eastern Europe's ethnic kaleidoscope,
but briefly there shone a Renaissance prince
in a place ill-suited for the event.
Contending between Sultan and Kaiser
and an array of secondary foes.
You continued what your father began;
For once fortune smiled on Pannonia.
Transient glory your sad legacy
library scattered to oblivion,
tomb desecrated, royal remains lost
subjects reduced to drinking "black soup".
But once the raven spread powerful wings,
soaring over river, mountains, and plains.

Her Eyes

Her eyes I remember most…
opened wide to capture
adolescent hopes and fears,
residual angst, concern
for others, nascent joys.

As time flowed,
as we touched
places and people
tangentially,
her eyes, older now
beheld fading dreams, wrong turns,
the what-might-have-beens
singing dirge-like melodies..

Angel, why was your hand not
upon her shoulder, why did you
not show a glimpse of glory
to saddened, tear-laden eyes?
Perhaps you did, but her eyes
saw what they wished to see.

For me, Angel, lift her eyes
beyond present concerns.
Raise them to the light
which will shine through them
again, sustaining them,
pointing them towards
endless bliss and not
previous struggles.

The Woman Who Knew Aldous Huxley

An informal gathering at someone's house
nestled in a Los Angeles canyon:
Over her walnut soup, Huxley's
razor-sharp Oxonian clarity
impressed her and her late husband.

A succession of images
surged through my mind
as she talked of Huxley:
reading the major novels
in high school library,
finding others at university
outside of classes and keg parties,
wandering through Central Europe
with German translation of
The Doors of Perception
(Die Pforten der Wahrnehmung)
and its mescaline-fueled mysticism
at the World's Biggest Drugstore.

Her long auburn hair wafted
in the Santa Ana winds
as we walked the neighborhood, she
a willowy figure infused with
ethereal qualities.

Before her daughter's birth
she had played jazz flute
and rode the Milky Way
a place of surrealism and tea
sprawling along the canals
in happening Amsterdam,

Several years earlier that flute
would have drawn me to her
for as long as she played.
But more permanence sought I
even if my thought was half-formed
my words ineffable.
No siren's call it was
sweetly singing to this wanderer
who already discerned from afar
another melody more compelling.

Briefly though it came faintly playing
as I read a post about Huxley
when the memory awakened
about the woman who knew Aldous Huxley.

One Morning You Will Decide

One morning you will decide
that this is the day to escape:

time to load the car, leave
the madness and mayhem.

Soon we will drive along
mesas, snow-capped mountains,

along the Natchez Trace
and the Appalachian chain.

Maybe we will leave the car
at the airport and fly to

that city on a cliff in Spain
you saw online or Vienna

where I will lure you to Sopron
and show you the family homestead.

Tell me when, my love, and I will
get the bags from upstairs.

The Archipelago

As the sun sets in the west
beyond the tall pine trees,
it simultaneously rises over
an archipelago amidst warm
Eastern waters.

No longer does that sun
shine in those dark, lively
eyes which once reflected
that light from shimmering sea
and spread over her visage.

Instead, these eyes behold
untold terrors and despair.
Tears rain down cheeks
which once glowed with joy.
Drawings depict the change
and descent into dark places.

Angel, burst the chains asunder,
unbind her eyes to gaze upon
the wonders awaiting her.
Gladden her pen, elate
her heart so she may once
more write of love and finally
bring light to those eyes,
to that visage, to that soul.

Aubade: The Bather

The lark rises: his song spreading
across the lake touched by dawn.
Cool water cupped in gentle hand
falls softly over her shoulders.
For a brief moment, she shimmers
in matinal, sun-kissed splendor.
Fortunate is the one who beholds
those long, damp tresses, seemingly-
chiseled countenance and torso,
glistening as though with colored
dewdrops flowing toward her breasts.

While Gazing at the Water

While gazing at the water
absorbed in my own thoughts,
a voice calls my name, clear
and lovely as a thousand chimes
 each caressed by a gentle breeze,
a whisper reaching a crescendo.

My eyes turn to the green field's
edge, where begins the grove.
Her smile like sunlight, she
calls again. Her eyes dancing
and shining upon my approach.

Everything once lost restored,
every care converted into joy.
In our embrace every moment
past, every moment to come
melts into an unending now.

The Sullen Expression of Growing Anger

The sullen expression glowers
from the back of the classroom,
glancing occasionally out of the window,
less frequently at the text
or the unfinished essay
rife with run-on sentences
and lacking punctuation.

I can tell you're not from here.
The words come my way
for no apparent reason.
They sound like a verdict
and become a barrier
to anything I have to offer about
 Atticus Finch, Langston Hughes.
or even myself.

What they think they glean
from meetings in deep forests
nocturnal internet surfing,
accusatory cable programming
and airwave pundits
pausing only for commercials.

His violence avoids danger.
In darkest night he will
firebomb a church where
he would be welcomed
in daylight hours.

When reality shatters their fantasy
the shards of broken glass
slice into innocent lives
and the sullen expression
dissolves far too late;

Kyrie, eleison   Lord, have mercy
Christe, eleison Christ, have mercy
Kyrie, eleison   Lord, have mercy

Idyll: The Shepherd and his Muse on Parnassus
Reflecting on the 2016 Election Campaign

Climb with me, my love, on Parnassus
and lie down close to me.
Listen closely; you can hear the
Republic of Cacophony.

Politicos, pundits, and all
united in conspiracy.
Their rants and raves fill the entire
Republic of Cacophony.

Better angels of our natures
to deaf ears make their plea
as we rapidly become a
Republic of Cacophony.

Let me place a flowery wreath
on your head, my love. Sing to me
sweet melodies drowning out that
Republic of Cacophony.

We Will Not Hear Words Like That Anytime Soon

While showing *the Writer's Almanac*
to young poets on 19 November, Lincoln's 272 words
of remembrance and resolution appeared.
How they rang and resounded over battlefield
and through classroom recitations, transcending
the solemn purpose that caused them to be spoken,
uniting a war-weary republic.

Where are the words
the majestic phrases
those sonorous cadences
sent forth in search of immortality?

They are lost in the din
of shrill leitmotifs
shouted regardless of all else,
Partisan diarrhea
obscuring all else
spoken only to be spoken.

They are unheard because
of the preference for reality shows
and paid advertisements
because half of us
know what we think anyway,
wisdom dispensed by
tailored suits and coiffured heads

We will not hear words like that anytime soon
in the future any iconic words
will require rebuttal directly underneath
or on a facing page.
Shrill hysterical lies repeated enough times
until they gain the semblance of truth
to the delight of a ghostly Goebbels
now resident in a bunker in hell.

The House on the Ridge

While wandering through life, I realized
most people had searched the horizon round
for that spot they desired more than others.
But still I gazed beyond beckoning hills.
From the lifting fog appeared on the ridge
the gleaming destination I long sought.
Gladly I settled into my new room.
Before too long, harsh redecoration
removed much of what I had come to love,
replacing them with things I could not stand.
Clutching what I could, searching other rooms,
eventually obtaining permission.
The best I achieved is rearranging
what I salvaged with what was already there...

Sonnet for All Saints Day

Annually attention focuses
on those beyond our communication.
Spaces imbued now with their silence,
hallowed for one or hallowed for many.
The consolation is we must not wait
that long; whenever necessary we
can commemorate them upon hearing
a certain song, seeing a photo or place.
Not yet can the dividing veil rise up
so that we now see as clearly as they.
But the veil acquires a translucency
allowing a glimpse of uncreated light.
For an instant, eternity flows through.
We behold in them what we shall become.

E'en's Last Dark Hour

Before e'en's last dark hour goes by.
Softly, my sweet, take I my leave of thee.
Like the wild geese now away I must fly.

Times of bliss we have savored, you and I.
As I leave, thy face, soft with sleep, I see
Before e'en's last dark hour goes by

Glimmering distantly in eastern sky
Helios rising over yonder tree.
Like the wild geese now away I must fly

Long embraced we two under moonlight sky
upon the lush green grasses of the lea
Before e'en's last dark hour goes by

Before falling asleep, I heard thy sigh,
beseeching me not to take leave of thee
Like the wild geese now away I must fly.

Before e'en's last dark hour goes by
and I the shining stars no longer see.
Beside thee, my love, I no longer lie.
Like the wild geese now away I must fly.

Lingering at Castalia

Along the banks of Castalia he sees
her waiting. Her hand lightly touching

the surface of cool, clear waters, eyes
looking beyond the mountain.

Softly, calling her name, delight
fills her face . She glows with warmth

of many stars. Rising, she reaches
him. They embrace on field of

sweet-smelling grass and speak
of verses, becoming each other's all.

Under billowing clouds they lie
in close contentment. Beholding

each other in a gaze that says
far more than can any words.

On Hearing Rachel Portman's "Cider House Rules"

Wistfulness and contentment
flow over me
whenever those tones
are played.

Long ago reading the book
watching the film
much later listening
on Klassik FM in
German hotel
her melodies reminded me
of what I left behind
and what awaited my return

From the keyboard's notes
soon enveloped by strings
and assorted reeds
halcyon tones invoke
peace and fulfilment
past present and future

Years later at book launch
the same notes resound
in an arts center
in a classroom
in my soul.

Quiet settles the horizon round,
blanketing forest and field, granting
some time for reflection.

Now is the quest almost concluded,
Strange places now become homeland.
Not all who sought remain.

In a flash realizing all along
I was not seeking every side
of many-sided Grail
but that what I found
was what I needed.

Having spent more than a dozen years in South Carolina, and eight of those in Saluda County, **Arthur Turfa** feels at home there. Originally from Pennsylvania, he has lived in California, New Mexico, and Virginia. His travels, studies, and military career have taken him around the world, especially to Germany, where he also has lived.

As a second-generation American; the Old Countries are never far from him, even though he is patriotic in the original sense of the word. Certain places are important to him because they have formed him even without his realizing it at the time. Later on he discovered connections between them that he never could have foreseen. People in each of those places have also influenced him,. Much of his poetry attempts to honor these people and to show the places to the reader.

Being bi-vocational before it was common, Turfa combines civilian and military ministry with teaching on secondary and post-secondary levels. These careers gave him countless insights and experiences, many of which are reflected in his poetry

As a young man he wrote poetry, but stopped in grad school and during his early professional life. During his 2004/05 deployment to Germany, he resumed writing poetry. Joanna Kurowska saw some of his early postings on Facebook and Google She told him that his poetry was good enough to be published. Turfa's poetry appeared in print and electronic journals in the United States and internationally, such as *SC English Teacher, altpoetics, Metaphor, Munyori Literary Journal, the Pangolin Review* and *Blue Streak.*

In 2015 *Places and Times* was released by eLectio Publishing. Two years later *Accents* came out, and is now on Amazon Desktop Publishing. *Gemini* appeared in 2018 from Broad River Books. *Saluda Reflections* was released in the Summer of 2018 by Finishing Line Press.

Turfa has also taught at Espanola Valley HS, Espanola, NM; Hazleton Area HS, Hazleton, PA; Gilbet HS, Gilbert, SC; Blythewood HS, Blythewood, SC; Luzerne County Community College, Nanticoke, PA; University of California-Irvine; Midlands

Technical College, Columbia, SC. A graduate of the Pennsylvania State University; he has also studied at the University of California-Berkeley; University of California-Irvine; Binghamton University; and Drew University. His professional organizations include the United States Army Reserve Component; American Association of Teachers of German' South Carolina Foreign Language Teacher Association (past president); National Council of Teachers of English He is an Owner at Words on Fire, and a past owner at POETS, Google+ poetry communities.

One thing he enjoys is mentoring newer and/or younger poets. When they are published somewhere, he shares there joy. His friendships with established poetry give satisfaction and inspiration.

After *Saluda Reflections* Turfa has another project or two in the planning stages, and looks forward to seeing them take form.

www.ingramcontent.com/pod-product-compliance
Lightning Source LLC
LaVergne TN
LVHW041557070426
835507LV00011B/1134